MW00982130

ORIENT

orient

Gillian Wigmore

brick books

BRICK BOOKS · 431 BOLER ROAD, BOX 20081
LONDON, ONTARIO N6K 4G6 · WWW.BRICKBOOKS.CA

Cover image, design and layout by Cheryl Dipede.
The author photo was taken by Melinda Roy.
This book is set in Arno Pro, designed by Robert Slimbach
and first issued by Adobe in 2007.

Library and Archives Canada Cataloguing in Publication

Wigmore, Gillian, 1976-, author
      Orient / Gillian Wigmore.
Poems.
ISBN 978-1-926829-92-0 (pbk.)
      I. Title.
PS8645.I34O75 2014   C811'.6   C2014-903903-4

We acknowledge the Canada Council for the Arts and the Ontario
Arts Council for their support of our publishing program.

for my parents

CONTENTS

SKYWARD FROM THE SELF • 9

RUSH EFFECT

Edmund de Waal's teapot of the metal handle • 25
mini ice age • 26
the appropriate weather • 27
the necrotizing Victorian fetish for lace • 28
vacation in Egypt • 29
ash paintings, art gallery of Ontario, June 2012 • 30
when we go to Spain • 31
work • 32
the truth • 33
birthday cowl • 34
the privilege is mine • 35

DITCH FLOWERS • 37

GROW

atlas of the mouth • 61
luckless, vinced • 62
mother of pearl • 63
song for February • 64
if you ever falter and stop loving • 65

song for March   • 67
city special   • 68
dear photograph   • 69
Vanderhoof girls   • 70
hewn   • 72
weather drawings   • 73
field notes   • 75

WHETHER THE WILDERNESS   • 77

NOTES   • 91
ACKNOWLEDGEMENTS   • 93
ABOUT THE AUTHOR   • 95

SKYWARD FROM THE SELF

1

the fact of a fish, a trout, a weighted thought,
firm, thick bend of flesh, flex of meat, heavy, unblinking, slick
fish of dreams, Plato's fish, lived for years in the black lake,
years, from fry to broken flesh.
this is no revelation, this smacked body-flinch,
and this is no poem of sorrow, not a flick of regret,
instead the flash of water flung skyward
from the self-preserving tail.

this perfect morsel, this unblemished self, this scathed or unscathed one
scaled green, gold, blue, black, pink, orange, grey, white, embolism of existence
cracked once, twice above the gills, centred thump on the hill above the eyes
like so – cease the ode, it's supper time.
beyond the silk gut, the gorgeous spleen, those
sated crows hanging around on the beach; beyond the memory
of weight in my arms, first as I pulled it forth and then as I held it close,
evening glare off the fading shine, dried slime, the fillet knife
catching the flash of light: after-image of the rod held high.

2

oh not just the fish, the fish, the fish –
also the poem of the fish,
the great spread of paper behind it, smoothed
so the crumples and crimps are just memories of folds gone wrong,
and the feeling about the fish is greater than the actual catch.

it's the dearness of it.
so busy loving the line from tail to dorsal fin.
the line enraptures me,
oh me. and where is the day in all this?
the rain gear, the drips off the ends of our noses.
we didn't kiss for fear of those drips but wanted to –
all exaltation for being out in it, the ice just off,
the boat seats so cold our bums were numb.
excuse me,

the light was an absence of light, the cold was greater than we let on.
the fish when we caught it was just one part of a day, the day is gone.

3

this too is false,
this preparation toward a mood
and how I add and add then change then subtract.
there were actual acrobats in the air,
swallows on the wing.

man low in the stern,
woman high in the bow.
motor on, they form a wake.
there is composition to consider.
there were swallows that defied beauty,
their motions so perfectly ordinary.

there is above the lake/below the lake,
the equation to consider,
the fraction of time spent in 'pause' on the page,
the effect of alliteration and rhyme.
does the swallow fly with beak open or does it snap
to swallow the fly? all on the arc, all with wings wide.

is it worth it? to categorize?
or does it wreck it?
we spent an afternoon fishing on freshly open water –
there was a swell on the lake and the birds
were never swallowed by the bulge of the water.
instead, with ever so slight a shift of wings, they soared.

4

loose recollection of sensation and voila!
revisited on paper, on screen, on retina, aloud,

and voice, the expression of gratitude, is inadequate because:
the cold liver, the cold blood, the cold spleen –

a guaranteed fail when faced with the fish as it is, as it was,
as I wrote it and lived it,
and the fish, the legendary, the imagined,

that death is the worst –
on the page, a retinal linocut,
or in your hands, cold and hard and clean.

5

gleam of flat light off the water bursts
when the sun breaks through

air between prow and water
a moment in which I am aloft

6

the romance of the fish:
mute
smooth

slick
indifferent

elusive
inhuman

7

cold hands in the water, washing off the viscera
of a winter spent underwater in the dark,
the bone ache of afterward.

cold eyes on a horizon half hidden by cloud,
fingers dripping, droplets falling
from the hands held just so above the water.

I watch I don't get blindsided by weather,
soaked by waves,
hooked off the earth from above by some sharp implement.

in slick blue raingear I'm freezing on shore,
spine a column of rocks stacked and shaken all day
by the rattle of the Evinrude.

I'm in love with the element,
the elemental, the element, the edges of the elements
where they meet: rock and water, water and air.

this is not wave spray, it's rain.
clenched toes in my gumboots.
there was bound to be retribution.

if the sun comes out can I take credit?
I wash the knife edge free of blood,
the curve of tempered steel and leather.

you did the dirty work
and we ate like kings.
the clouds broke eventually and turned the lake black.

8

pyre on the beach
and fish on the fire in a black pan.
night falling.

this part didn't happen.

after the weather, the hole in the atmosphere
where finally we can breathe,
and the fish, out of its element, drowns.

fire on the beach.

fish on the pyre in a black pan with butter
and it's quiet without the wind,
the water lapping now.

trade in the fleshed fish for the fish in the pan,
sizzle of butter in exchange
for the stiff dorsal fan of the fin, the gills,

the fish, fresh-eyed,

fast in the green dark,
too fast to imagine –
the sparks off the fire against the sky,

the flick of the finger, the tail,

the fast fish gone in the green under
the miles and miles of lake, away,
a flash of silver then only dreams.

the distance
between real and written,
between capture and dinner,

the tale and the articulated tail.

9

and this perfect morsel, this unblemished self,
the unscathed one: gone
beyond, the crows, unsatisfied, hanging around on the beach
and me with the memory of a weight in my arms,
first as I pulled it forth and then as I held it close.

the fillet knife caught the flash of light.
I held the rod high.
the image of a fish, a trout
and then? a weighted thought
but no revelation, no poem of sorrow, no flick of regret.
instead the flash of water flung skyward
from the self-preserving tail.

heavy, unblinking
slick fish of dreams, oh
sing the ode, it's suppertime –
evening glare off the fading shine.

RUSH EFFECT

Edmund de Waal's teapot of the metal handle

coming to the lip of the pot instead of turning
you end   and ending you edge delicate and thin
unapologetically abrupt and imperfect and thus   slim wall
ever so slightly blue but also sea foam green   crazed
round the body of the pot like steam unreleased
          the inside affects the outside   there
you cut the line and affix a handle like the wire that hems
the cattle in   a handle unforgiving
clasping itself and the pot so beautifully   strand
by strand wound silver so totally certain   imagine tea
from such a pot   its slender arcing neck
taste the tannin that won't ever stain its skin

mini ice age

the train to Skagway offers questions ranging from groundcover type
to railway bridge construction, from *what do we call the colour of the
velvet skin sloughing off a caribou antler?* to *wouldn't caribou make good
coat racks?* to *mum, would you love me less if I shed my skin like a snake?*
and travelling cold over clackety clack clack and the windrush, the
stink of train through a tunnel while we ride over hold-your-breath
holes in the earth the tracks cross, imagine travel by foot carrying
ONE METRIC TONNE of gear (or: one ton of gear because now
we're in America), I experience three years later a mini ice age of faith
because I ran past a church called Church of Overcoming Faith, like it
was a road block or an affliction, but also because I can't bear this heat,
I'm not strong enough to withstand climate change whilst being brave
or showing bravado or lying: *yes, my darling, I'd love you even if you shed
your skin like a snake, in fact I'd love you more.*

the appropriate weather

the appropriate weather holds
the cold near the surface of the earth,
stills the wind in the leaves for rush effect
that startles. the weather,
like a lover, smothers the pores
of sensation so no single feel
escapes whole – and so the rain
threatens: in softest greys, most promising
blues and aching white on white on white,

and here, bearing the weather
like an anvil, we wait
for some other avenue, some
release, the sinuses
clogged with remorse or anger or
breathless, senseless fear.

the necrotizing Victorian fetish for lace

I'm not going to try to force it but let me just.
no to polar bears, penguins, assumptions, a coast guard with no arms or armament
and ask me this: is it hard, your art? not as opposed to soft,
but to explain?

who gets the final word anyway?
the rolled-oat version.
we're waiting for it: spring, low water, aspen to bust out
in one body, aflame.

get wind of it.
she posted higher each stride, each haunch bunch and stretch, black hat gleaming.
it's not about the big picture, the stabbing pain behind your eye;
it's about the big picture.

vacation in Egypt

when Greg was on the bridge in Cairo his camera
followed the arc of smoke bombs and tear gas
canisters smacked the concrete and bounced into the river.
a man tried to start a chant.
men in riot gear, flak pants and helmets
made a roughly drawn line that broke the bridge
into Here and There and the chant was taken up,
tossed in failed volleys like tear gas canisters.
a man was hit in the arm with one.

that wasn't on camera.
who knows what that looked like?
we can imagine the impact after propulsion –

Greg's eyes teared and ran and the man with the chant
tried again and again until his words were passed
mouth to mouth across the bridge and reached
the silky inner ears of the other Egyptians
with their weapons and vests
blocking the bridge in Cairo.

ash paintings, art gallery of Ontario, June 2012

incense ash from Buddhist temples,
sorted, white through black,
then sifted onto canvas,
enough to call up heartache:
ash paintings of men swimming through mud,
arms held high, faces blurred,
their dusty guns kept dry overhead.

a hush in the gallery
after the artist's smoky toil –
men with blank smudges for eyes,
a woman in the field, her incense-ash hat –
a moment to pause and react.

this is enough for a minute
to make us all more human –
because we burnt prayers,
because we remember war –

enough for the moment,
and I can walk away from the grey
into the white light of afternoon –
a cheer from Little Italy, England up by one.
beer blackens the asphalt, a heavy wet heat –
a breath of wind lifts the tang of smoke from my skin,
but the whiff of it,
the grit remains within.

when we go to Spain

and the chk chk sprinklers wake us
dropping water like rain on the tent fly
calling us out to shuck off our husks and fly,
and the dry hours of driving are ahead of us,
imagined as yet, we will drink our coffee
and eat our bread.

like Arizona, it beckons hot and windy,
and I can't concentrate for all the pining after cacti
and guava juice, hot little shots
of coffee in the morning – I'm coughing up winter
like a bad cold. remember? there were gales, dry skin
cracked, glazed skies over the frozen earth.

like Antigua, Argentina, like Ibiza, unlike here,
when we rise, in Spain, to the sweet, sere morning
we'll sigh and be still for once. let me cry a little –
hot coffee in the hot morning, water drops
like little bomb blasts in the dust on the hilltops.

work

lift off the pot lid of the sky and find underneath
humans grubbing at the threshold of air.

one small caterpillar retreats from my eyes,
absconds, rearward, into the tube he's made of the leaf.

here are two things to care for: what you think
and what you know. the rest is excavation and de-scaling.

the truth

from the office the highway is all sirens, stops and starts,
whistles and lights, jake brakes and the rumble
that gets me in the gut and lower:
a small spot of arousal in a daily kind of day.

grey and white and stark, naked trees, snow
truncating the traffic as it zooms past then stops
then goes again on the green – if
I were a different woman I'd find a metaphor.

honestly, I only look every other day to see
if I can see the accident that calls the flock
of fire trucks and the ambulance, attend
instead to the details of desk top and finger taps.

truth is, the traffic goes and sometimes
I'm the traffic. it's my car zipping past
the window I'm not in because I am on the highway,
wipers flashing, destination: roam.

birthday cowl

your mother doubles the wool with other wool.
five hundred miles away she draws a line,
and afterward I draw a line too but don't think to underline it.
she's not here and I don't scrub the bathtub.

I borrow you from my younger self for just a minute
to dig up a frisson of jesus yes from our first kiss.
the lines around us were concrete and undergrad,
definitive but unfinished – we made our own.

I told your mother I fear you'll leave me, and her horror-face
matched my horror-face and the day was marred with my thoughts
despite your eloquence on the soccer field: you were thirty-five years old.
acknowledge the thought, she said, and let it go. I did.

I have an us on loan from future selves I consult for lines
around the mouth and wrinkles further to the wrinkles we already wear,
and I love us. I cart us around for comfort, for reference,
but I don't clue in we are motherless, though we will be by then.

I acknowledge the thought and love your mother from afar
by washing the bathtub, by drawing a line in deep around our family.
I draw on her drawings of you as a boy to feed my love,
and I wear her love for me: a cowl in grey, underlined with blue.

the privilege is mine

each strand of glitter in an othertime black beard,
each crack at the eye edge,
the sparklers of fifteen years.

then, when we come home, each mug I culled yet saved
because it wasn't mine to dispose of,
each cup of tea is a gift: heat and milk.

later, when we're wisps
of dry white memory floating in our empty house,
at least we had this: me learning finally to light the barbeque,

you with dental floss at the mirror,
you with your feet hanging off the bed,
you with your smile, leaning over me, and what we said.

DITCH FLOWERS

strut

loose-pegged legs and arms flappin
fast walkin past the co-op card lock
past the corner
down the highway
the feedstore, the sweet stink
of wet grain and baby chicks
cross the tracks
up Stewart too damn haunted
with old houses not damn there anyway
come to the lights and full stop

jig a bit
jig a bit
jig and jig and jig a bit
the Reid's open
beer

cowboy poetry

I never needed a rhymin dictionary
kept a runnin list down the left margin
words stacked up like springboards
on the right, chute and toot
bird and word, spring sky
and the long long way down Lily Valley Road
to the brother's place
and spayin heifers in the old chute
binder twine and balin wire weldin
the whole lot of us together
toots of rum before breakfast
for the long morning scarin cattle
down the fence, ridin horse
spittin chew
rue
that rhymes with chew

drunk on remembrance day

left the legion before the others, shufflin a little, slurrin a little
no words left standin
just the whispers that do get out –
it's the damn poetry again, like a disease

beer and poetry, wet coasters and horse piss
no regret
left standin
like a pigeon in the rain

no one cares about the damn poppies
bald pates and horned hands, the spit line
like a spider web from pipe stem to shakin spotted lips

Lucy jig on saturday night

mmm mmm oh oh
mmmm mmm oh oh
lucy jig onna saturday night
lucy jig onna saturday night
mmm mmm oh oh
mmm mmm oh

in here somewhere

it's in here somewhere, that bottle, I know it, hid it last week or a week and a half ago, I know I did, I know I got it somewhere

in here somewhere, in the rubble, jesus christ, I don't know how it gets like this, clothes and boots, boots and toots and root beer bottles, jesus christ

it's in here somewhere, I know I hid it, I gotta find it, oh my christ I ask so little, I ask so little, just write it down, you say, pray, you say, you don't know shit, it's in here somewhere

my heart, in here somewhere, lay hands on me, in here somewhere, I'm in here searchin and it's vain, vain searchin, lord, that bottle, it's with a pen, got lost together

hat

got this hat in Grand Cache
watched the bull ropin all day
did a couple rounds as a clown

ask anybody they'll tell you
I'm a genius in the ring
I know right when
the bottom of the barrel's
the right place to be

gals

Lu-ann: liquor store
Sue: co-op
Cindy: feed store
Harmony: video store
Lisa: pizza place
Harmony, nope. did her already
Amber: cross-walk lady
Sheila: emergency
Jen and Stacey: cold beer and wine
Violet: pharmacy
Mrs. Dr. Albegheny: clinic
old Mrs. Wheeler: old folks' home
Laila: bar
Cecilia: olden days, tavern

tavern

nobody says tavern any more
just pub or bar – you can't say poetry
in a pub or bar
you can say whatever you want to in a tavern

one night, the power out
I told a poem no one's heard
the like of before or since

me either since I made it up
in the dark, words bubblin up
like clams in mud

breakin the surface like so much
air, but all these men –
mill men, cowboys, vagrants, farmers –

I had them silent
I had them still, I had words
comin out of me like nothin

I ever knew before
or since
there's been drought and flood

they've closed the mill
and opened it again
I had a job and then I didn't

but once I spoke a tavern sermon
that came to me in darkness
and men I knew who crossed the street

who shunned me in daylight
they wept
and that's somethin

loose

can't keep my eyes steady
like they're floatin sans moorin
got this feelin in my olly-ohs
like they're swimmin in eye juice
if the guys notice, they look away

Pete's got this belt buckle I always liked
abalone sky, inset silver steer
I watch his middle to pin my eyes
to somethin solid, Pete's middle
my eyes swimmin back and forth
and weepin now, for chrissake
weepin, now Pete's leavin
can't stand me starin all wet
and fuckin hopeless

singin

after ridin
after brandin
after a week in camp
after open heart surgery
after pain or toothache
after death
after the drum roll
after after afternoon
late at night: Cecilia
oh my heart singin

too much, too many

rodeo clown was the best, but I did bridge work too, smoothin concrete
and washin trucks. talked up the lady in the first aid camper, but she
had me fired. said I was too familiar.
worked drivin truck, but it was awful. lonely. too dull to last. spent too
much time at the lunch counter at the husky fill-ups, too much time
talkin, too many times wakin up in the dawn with the side of my face
stuck to the wall of the shitter, the floor of a truck, the back of some
lady's hand. spent too much time not drivin. didn't last two seasons.
spent a winter in the Sault not workin, just thinkin about it and home.

home

home's this dirty rag
this saggin couch, this almost toothless comb
home's this stained road
this double-high load, this stupid achin cold
I can't shake, hackin and hackin
muckin up the poems

home's this poem
and that one and the cold glass on the bar
it's the almost beer with almost everyone
whose mothers I knew
back before they ran off with Seymour

home you son of a bitch
you righteous cunt, you war-mongerin mormon
you whore's son, you wantin
sore-eyed dirty beggar
you trailer full of nothin
you want

home was Susan
home was home
home was almost Susan
oh jesus, remember her jam
her fat lovin arms before winter

I never meant no harm
I gummed it up
I sold my home for six pints and rollies
to smoke tobacco I won in poker
home's this wantin home
so bad it sucks my soul dry
breathin in
and pukes it up on the out breath

beer with the mayor

back when he was the mayor's boy and small town dynasty
was somethin ignorable he said
'lord don't you say some sweet shit, man'
and didn't I?
and the small town dynasty is somethin they talk about
in circles and half-a-misms because it's too damn obvious
to be astute about
he said 'lord, man, you shouldn't drink so much'
and that too was obvious but he bought me another
and I told about this valley back before it was mechanized
and the grass was waist-high in the middle of town
and I sounded astute and well brought up
then I thought about that and cried for my mother
he said 'you're a piece a work, man'
and I always was and said so
then he became the mayor
and where the train tracks cross the river I told a poem
about my heartburn, usin chalk and language
like the ditch flowers, so pretty at the end of summer
then dead and unwanted
I used spray paint and swear words
and he became the mayor
he bought me beer in 1970
then locked me up for mischief
astute indeed

hole in the absolute bottom of the bottom

lower than lower than lower than low
that's where the bottom is
that's where I go
ho-low, how low? back out to Stoney Creek
and down to the slow
flow
Nechako
long ago
when it mattered

damn

damn I knew I was gonna do somethin big
when I was a kid, somethin huge, somethin wonderful

damn I did a thing or two when I was rootin tootin
back when I was wonderful

woo-wee but I damn was carburetin wonderful
when I think about it *damn*

but I was good back in the day
and dammit the nights was even better

last call

I love every part of this town es-
peshally the sidewalk

lay here with me, won't you?
we can watch the stars go round

akimbo

sometimes you haul yer own self up by the hair
of your nards because you can't just lie there
even if it was a bad night
you grab them hairs and pull
you shake your head and tell yourself
this old world won't make its own poetry
you son of a bitch you get up
and make some poetry
make some wonderful thing that surprises everyone
you included
you just get up and jig
you old wet clown
get in the ring
get in the river
get your old self walkin down Prince George Hill
till you can't feel your feet
and yer just jiggin
and jiggin
and feelin that itchy beat tumble home
down the hill to town
and it lays there awaitin for you
because you
are its only lovin son

GROW

atlas of the mouth

tongue the space
in the holy hall
full of teeth
and gums and spit
honour it:
say us, here, this

luckless, vinced

darker outline of the mountains
dark blue of the sky
minus the stars
out this left window on the universe
            bpNichol, *Continental Trance*

we aren't the sum of the length of time it took to get here, nor the wail
of train hauling track down east and away, we aren't and weren't.
we got here and it hurt, there was sunset, the darker outline of the mountains,

me and you,
the sky dark blue.

if this life is a journey we are worn raggedy, blaspheming non-stop,
vigour lost, laces fucked in knots, we tried and tried and tried, we waited
luckless, vinced after being invincible, when once the sky was ours.
now this: night minus all stars.

we are sweating, breathless, the air travelling in and down
down down to all our necessary organs and once
I loved you –
            all this and us stopping at McBride Station
in the perfect v, the direct cunt of the valley. I wanted to be
your vital statistics, your emergency services, I wish we mattered.

there are tracks and wilderness and nothing else
left out this window on the universe.

mother of pearl

what have we got like mother of pearl?
oceans and light.
you have abalone and oyster, exotic
cups of sky and salt.
we have duff and scree, the wind in advance of a storm,
the dacron blue of June bearing down.

what have we got like mother of pearl?
light, golden inches between birches,
filtered evening light off the lake, the wait
for night, the hot scent of summer
overcome by winter,
cold, indifferent, nacreous:
sun on snow.

song for February

half inch of water under the snow, so
broken the crust gives
and the prints of dog, crow, girl
and mother are black holes of go
in the half dark, in the long night
of winter's inelegant unravelling,
walk after walk
until dog shit permeates the air
in some far off, gentler, better time.

behold me almost giving up,
almost kneeling down in the slurry
of past people gone, their wreck of the path
remaining, trampled proof of what? a winter?
the impetus springs – sausages
broiled over tomatoes from Mexico,
rosemary, beets – I could transform these
with the heat of the oven
into what? love? hope? maybe.
I raise my eyes and walk,
the goad of her hand in mine.

if you ever falter and stop loving

this curious line that runs the circle round my navel then extends
in rays outward, seventy rays, eighty rays, silver, segmented, pink
sometimes, rays shining up toward my head, out toward my arms, down
toward my legs.

if you ever falter and stop loving the city, the stupid starts and stops, the
roads to nowhere, the half-built roundabouts abandoned and the paths
along the ridge tops, the grass in the meridian, the blood on George St.,
the river,

and if you ever falter and stop loving this particular cul-de-sac, the
driveway, those unruly roses and the transplanted stonecrop,

don't tell me.

if you ever answer no to love and falter to a stop and love instead the
answers better than the questions like: is the sun? yes. the roses? no.
are we there yet?

don't answer that.

love, love the questions, the where of the meandering lines, the heat
at the centre of the rays, my long, long elongated navel that begs the
question: what happened here?

I'll tell you: love.

don't falter, grow:

in the holes in the cracks in the sidewalks, in the gaping booths where
public phones once hung, in the gaps between the old me and the new
me, love the graceless line, love, the shooting stars, the rays leading
up, down and home, don't stop

song for March

indoors the aunties tend the seedling trays, safe from frost and the
scraping action of sky, the wide, side-balanced blue through the
window, clouds on the run. the wind sends the new shoots grovelling.

we're shit-smeared from boots to hat brim. the soft brown of coveralls
lost in the crust of cow plop from barnyard clambering, roping on the
fly to track the wild calvers down.

more of this, please: scabs of snow on the dirt piles, road-edge fireweed
dried out and rasping,
armies of new pine in the fields and tea to come in the late afternoon.
for now, bright sun, chapped skin – March on the central plateau.

city special

broken baluster canted east
and stuck, point up amongst the sheetrock
and glass, the glitter in the grass,
the failed foundation, the concrete
chunked up and useless – in this
a field mouse builds a mouse house
of dry grass and fabric remnants, string,
strips of brown cassette tape in the rain
that sparkles with the passing light of car
headlights and street lamps –

it's this we overlook: the special
in the dirt, the mouse and the magpie's version,
the crow wheeling overhead
on the lookout for carrion and chips.

dear photograph

I don't feel nostalgic so much
as I feel sick, as the autocorrect
capitalizes the initial letter of each line
like a tic: a reminder that tells me
I'm not right, not perfect,
no longer four feet tall.

all I want is a reminder
not to feel nostalgic/a trick
knee that fails each time I falter
and reach back for something that wasn't
as I imagined it. I self-correct, I edit
each time I slip.

Vanderhoof girls

after Charles Lillard

sometimes you think of her and her shotgun wedding,
her dad dancing barefoot till his footsteps bled.
you think of her and you think of her sister,
who married a mormon elder when they were both fifteen
and she was the prettiest, smartest girl in the school
before she disappeared and before you thought seriously
of burning the whole thing down, then left instead.

you think of her giant farm truck and apples and peanut butter,
Simon and Garfunkel blaring from popped speakers,
the two of you singing and the road grass all burnt up and hopeless.
you think of her mum, who was quiet and worked with troubled youth,
and then you think of her with her eyes brimming,
the both of you standing dumb in the foyer of the friendship centre
holding eyes, not hands, because her mum was thrown from a horse, killed,
and you knew no other motherless girl your same age.

you stop thinking because it hurts.
you've spent too much time and words on landscape.
you owe them more, you've been pretending you don't belong
but all along you've known: you're her,
no matter your travels, your schooling, your poems.
you know her too well – her and her and you.

it's self-preservation, all this writing, reminding yourself
where you're not, where you could be,
where you'll finally be: the plot of land above the hospital
your great-grandad bought in 1925 to house the whole ramshackle lot of you
when you die. You lie staring, wide eyes to the ceiling,
remembering, fearing falling to earth, succumbing to the current,
to some hometown boy, or some good old-fashioned home birth
in Vanderhoof, two miles from the family homestead.

hewn

here, in the tumble home from sky
to cliff to curve, we meet the inward-seek
of cave hollow, black and chamois yellow,
brown, dust, and if we look,
a chalky shade of blue.

the armoire of cool after sun,
shade after heat. note
the greys after the blues.
we seek the fall
from home, above ground,
to below,

from beams and boards and wood
to the shiff of moving soil,
the smooth-packed earth floor –
this is what we're after:
abode of before-thought,
when the dark was all around us,
and in the dark we built a fire.

weather drawings

crows made projectiles of the wind's

slick green raincoat rubber
(my husband before he was my husband
        walking toward me)

let me in and also me

not pretty
not even caring to be pretty

overwhelming and unapologetic

blasting pea gravel right out of the driveway
wearing the corners off buildings

like a photograph
but different
        quieter

hopeful but how?

exclusive

the relief of the multitudes
        yes multitudes

looking in, looking out, looking in, looking out

that's all – sun
on the bald spot
so hard on the forearms it hurts

burning refrain

truth and also the glare off Africa

blunt
repeating

field notes

in the field and not notes but notes
like those struck from a piano
that dissipate soon as they're sung

it needs to be faint
it needs to be fleeting
I need to be not in it

only a suggestion of inhabitation
a faint track, three lines
and a fourth

umber only
and here
let it lift from the page

Whether the wilderness is
real or not
depends on who lives there.

—Margaret Atwood,
Journals of Susanna Moodie

WHETHER THE WILDERNESS

cabin on fire

she drinks tea on the porch
impervious to the inferno

real or not? depends
who sees it burn

**the petals of the fire-
weed fall where they fall**

she says nothing, stares me in
squat by the fire, her knees flared out
the fire between them, pot
in front of that

scent off her like moss
dried cedar fronds when she wafts past
to reach in the high dark
hidden spaces in the corners of her cabin

a flash of intimacy that hasn't happened
I can taste the cinnamon grizzly
skin under the hair
at the back of her neck

she grunts and juts her chin at me
the thicket of her locks
like a dark shawl around her
eyes like dry tinder: *what do you want?*

**the trail was not
among the trees but
the trees**

deadfall and underbrush
thick and overgrown
bugs torrential
why struggle on?
for tea?

I can see her on the dock
though I've never seen her
casting a line like a question
over the water: *now? now?*
drops it down like a sighed answer:
now

strike if you dare
she looks my way even
though she doesn't

**I am a word
in a foreign language**

an unused word

she lifts her head when I step inside
I thought myself here
thought the path into existence
the leaves a wilderness I had to execute
to find her warm hovel
thick fug of stew

she lifts the hem of her skirt
when I come inside
wipes my face
with loose-weave cloth
licks me clean
with a dirty tongue

she doesn't like me, but she'll wash me
before I foul her
and I do

**between the jagged edge
of the forest and the jagged river**

mosquitos in the shadows, wet heat and sucking mud
two options: go forward, go back

stifling fronds and sticking burrs
the river's no better – rocks

and froth, boils and holes
and in this no man's land: her

beckoning, waving me off
sweating and panting, I waver on the cusp

**(each refuge fails
us; each danger
becomes a haven)**

if this is a new land
I disembark here

my boat ill-conceived
badly executed

I relieve myself of myself
as a sailor

I'm a wayfarer now
whether or not I'm wanted

if this is love, I want off
if the question is the answer

I'll take it
step by bracken-bound step

by thicket, by thistle
this will do because I choose

not the usual, not the everyday
not what we guess at

and get right
I'm smacked in the face

with root stench and mushroom funk
punishment of trees

yes, this, please

surrounded, stormed, broken
in upon by branches, roots, tendrils, the dark

droplet by droplet, black and viscous
suckled by illicit liquor meted out
on offer only
because I am a squally baby
having given up my wits
to this old hag

hold me close

she does
and I go down past the roots
into wormland, scuttling bug
territory of reaching
white hairs secreting air
even as they suck sugar
from the earth

pretend this dirt is the future

I do, I do
oh god, I do
I can't not, I want it
I deserve this
I do

don't think, don't hope
don't fall for it, go
she's waiting
and she's waiting
but it's I
who, I

go down to the road edge
go past the burnt tree
wallow in it
the ditch growth
the mud, the bile

charred marks
now around which I
try to grow

imagine the burn
before the blueberries come back
before fireweed forgives
the land with its abundance

imagine the black trunks
and sloughed bark
the dark trough of earth
scored and rent
but quiet

before aftermath
before regrowth
this other choosing
a second chance
at manhood

I hack a trail
through overgrowth
headed slow
head down
headed home

NOTES

All titles from "**whether the wilderness**" are from Margaret Atwood's *Journals of Susanna Moodie*. With thoughts toward Emily Carr, Susanna Moodie, Margaret Atwood and D'Sonoqua.

Thanks to Elisabeth de Mariaffi for housing me during "**ash paintings, art gallery of Ontario, June 2012.**"

"**weather drawing**" and "**field notes**" are after Alexis Rockman's *Weather Drawings*.

"**city special**" thanks to Sachiko Murakami as a renovation for *Project Rebuild* (www.projectrebuild.ca), and for Prince George.

"**birthday cowl**" is for Colleen Couves.

Travis Sillence knows which poems are for him.

"**Vanderhoof girls**" is written in response to Charles Lillard's "Vanderhoof" from *Circling North* (Sono Nis Press, 1988) and was first published as a broadside by Companions Series (High Ground Press, 2009). With love to Rebecca Verduzco.

Versions of some of these poems appeared, sometimes in different form, in the following magazines: *filling station*, *The Malahat Review*, *The Fiddlehead*, *Event* and *The Puritan*. I'm grateful to the editors for their support. Poems from this book were also published in *Force Field: 77 BC Women Poets* (Mother Tongue Publishing, 2013).

ACKNOWLEDGEMENTS

I'm grateful for the support of my community, my friends and, especially, my family: Travis, Elly and Emmett Sillence.
I'm thankful to live and write where I do, in north-central BC, with the support of so many generous people.
Thank you to my editor, Stan Dragland, and to everyone at Brick Books.